The Award-Winning Series
SIR KAYE THE BOY KNIGHT Book 1

THE KNIGHTING OF SIR KAYE

DON M. WINN

The Award-Winning Series
SIR KAYE THE BOY KNIGHT Book 2

THE LOST CASTLE TREASURE

DON M. WINN

The Award-Winning Series
SIR KAYE THE BOY KNIGHT Book 3

LEGEND OF THE FOREST BEAST

DON M. WINN

ELDRIDGE CONSPIRACY

DON M. WINN

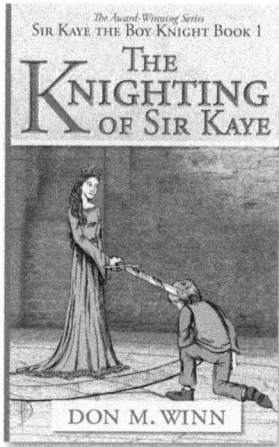

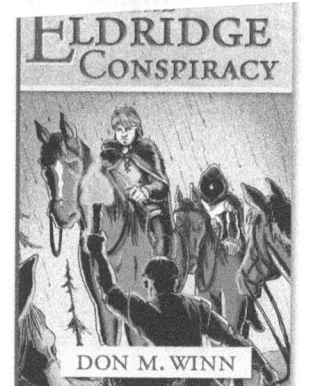

Study Guide for the
Sir Kaye the Boy Knight Series
by Don M. Winn

Contributors:
Don Winn
Elizabeth Winn
Jade LaRue West
Elizabeth Bowers

Illustrations by
Dave Allred

Study Guide for The Sir Kaye the Boy Knight Series Copyright © 2017 Don M. Winn
Developed by Don Winn, Elizabeth Winn, Jade La Rue West, and Elizabeth Bowers
All rights reserved.
ISBN: 978-1-937615-39-0
Published 2017 by Cardboard Box Adventures Publishing

www.donwinn.com

The Knighting of Sir Kaye © 2012 Don M. Winn
All rights reserved.
ISBN: 978-1-937615-19-2

The Lost Castle Treasure © 2014 Don M. Winn
All rights reserved.
ISBN: 978-1-937615-31-4

Legend of the Forest Beast © 2016 Don M. Winn
All rights reserved.
ISBN: 978-1-937615-32-1

The Eldridge Conspiracy © 2017 Don M. Winn
All rights reserved.
ISBN: 978-1-937615-35-2

Table of Contents

Sir Kaye the Boy Knight Book One: The Knighting of Sir Kaye, paired with the Book 1 Lesson Plan, offers a fun and engaging story while providing a great introduction to medieval literature. Together, the book and lesson plan expand vocabulary and spelling skills and can be used to teach life lessons to help students both in and out of the classroom. The lesson plan focuses on central themes that students can apply to their lives, like the importance of bravery, the proper way to deal with jealousy, and how pride can keep people from doing the right thing.

Sir Kaye the Boy Knight Book Two: The Lost Castle Treasure is a suspenseful and mysterious story sure to keep your students on the edge of their seats. Paired with the lesson plan, this is a perfect way to introduce new creative writing techniques. In daily lessons, students are shown that there are many ways to express emotion through writing and actions. Drawing from the text and enjoying acting fun, your class will learn to think creatively about ways emotions can be conveyed. Students are challenged to write their own sentences describing feelings, driving home the lesson and inspiring creativity.

Sir Kaye the Boy Knight Book Three: Legend of the Forest Beast is an adventurous installment in the series portraying complex and relatable characters while teaching kids that they are capable of great things. The story and lesson plan teach the importance of humility while challenging their creative and objective writing skills. Beginning with fun trivia to test reading comprehension, the lesson plan also provides activities to help students create their own fictional characters and questions to stimulate comprehensive classroom discussions about what humility looks like in contemporary life. Vocabulary activities help students improve dictionary and writing skills.

Sir Kaye the Boy Knight Book Four: The Eldridge Conspiracy is the exciting conclusion to the series. With an adventure that teaches loyalty, friendship, and determination, the lesson plan teaches critical thinking skills for reading fiction and demonstrates ways to be loyal and trustworthy friends. The writing intensive lesson plan challenges your students to write their own similes, learning new ways to express their feelings. Vocabulary activities help students integrate new words into everyday language.

What was life like in the Middle Ages? Supplemental materials help students enjoy an immersive experience while reading the Sir Kaye series. Historical material and drawings provide a frame of reference for students to understand a lifestyle so different from today's, while offering numerous opportunities for class projects.

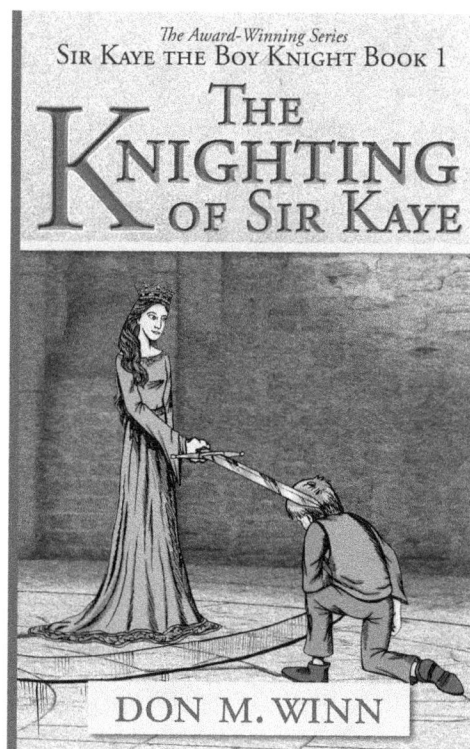

The Knighting of Sir Kaye

Back of Book Description: Kaye is an ordinary boy who dreams of becoming a legendary knight like his absent father. When the new queen knights Kaye for doing a brave deed to help another person, he gets his wish a lot sooner than he expected...but he's got a lot to live up to. Can he hold his own against all the other knights who hate him? Can he outwit the terrible Sir Melchor and defeat him in the deeds-at-arms competition in which all knights in the kingdom must participate? Can he help the queen save her kingdom...even a little bit?

Reading Comprehension Game

Split the class into two teams and keep score on the board, or don't have teams and offer individual students a prize (piece of candy, sticker, etc.) when he or she gets a trivia question right.

- What does Reggie lose toward the beginning of the story? *His father's compass*
- What is Kaye's Father's name? *Sir Henry*
- Does Reggie have any siblings? *No*
- Does Kaye have any siblings? *Yes, little sister Meg*
- What is the name of Kaye's village bully? *Charles*
- What is the name of the woods the boys explore? *The Knotted Woods*
- What is the real name of Meg's horse? *Cider*
- What do Kaye and Reggie find in the village bully's hideout? *Wooden carvings*
- What did Reggie call Charles' secret hideout? *A beaver hut*
- What does Kaye tell Reggie the name Kadar means? *Strong*
- What does Reggie chase at the beginning of the story? *A fox*
- What special skill does Kaye use to get Reggie out of the quicksand? *Knitting*
- What does Reggie's father do for a living? *Wool Merchant*
- Who taught Kaye how to knit? *His grandfather*
- What does Meg rename her horse? *Kadar*
- What does Reggie find buried in the woods? *A helmet*
- What is Kay's mother's name? *Lady Martha*
- What is Reggie's favorite food? *Meat pie*

Introduction to a Main Theme: Jealousy

- Introduce the class to the idea of jealousy by first asking if anyone can give a definition of the word.
- Write a basic definition of jealousy on the board.
  Jealousy: an unhappy or angry feeling of wanting to have what someone else has.
- Ask the students to give an example of what jealousy looks like.
  When a friend has something new (game, pet, phone, tablet) that you wish you had
  When you feel a sibling is receiving more attention than you
- Ask if anyone has any examples of when they have been jealous.
- Ask students how they feel when they are jealous. *Angry, Upset, Sad, etc.*
- Ask if any students can give examples from the story of when a character is acting jealous.
  Page 27: Reggie is jealous of Kaye's friendship with Charles and worries that Kaye would rather be with Charles than him.
  Page 28: Charles does not want to be friends with Kaye anymore because he is jealous of Kaye having a father because his own father ran away.
  Page 42: Meg renames her horse Kadar because she is jealous that Kaye's horse might be stronger than her own or because she is jealous for the attention that Kaye's fine horse gets.
- Steer the class towards these examples (or other examples from the book) and then ask if there is a better way for the characters to have reacted, instead of out of anger or envy.

Introduce Vocabulary for Entire Book

Introduce students to the vocabulary words they will see throughout the story and have the class copy the words down onto note cards. Or, for dictionary practice, give students the list of words and have them look up the words for themselves. The following definitions are from the Merriam-Webster Dictionary.

Ransom: (n.) money that is paid in order to free someone who has been captured or kidnapped

Witty: (adj.) funny and clever

Tapestry: (n.) a heavy cloth with designs or pictures woven into it that is used for wall hangings, curtains, etc.

Goblet: (n.) a container used for drinking liquids that has a round bowl on top of a stem attached to a flat base

Astounding: (adj.) causing a feeling of great surprise or wonder

Mentor: (n.) someone who teaches or gives help and advice to a less experienced and often younger person

Rebel: (n.) a person who opposes or fights against a government

Foul: (adj.) very unpleasant to taste or smell

Sulk: (v.) to be angry or upset about something and to refuse to discuss it with other people

Bellow: (v.) to shout in a deep voice

Reading Comprehension Game

Like in part one, create a game to test students on reading comprehension by asking trivia questions.
  • How many robbers were there? *Six*
  • What are three adjectives that describe the robbers? *Answers may vary*
  • What were three of the robbers' names? *Rex, Crimson, Badger*
  • Which bandit is wearing Reggie's compass? *Rex*
  • What skill does Kaye use to defeat the bandits? *Knitting*
  • Who did Kaye and Reggie save from the bandits? *Beau*
  • Who is Beau's aunt? *The queen/ Queen Vianne*
  • What trail was Beau riding on when he was robbed? *The Perilous Trail*
  • Where do Kaye and Reggie hide to spy on the bandits? *In a tree*
  • What do Kaye and Reggie nickname Alfred the messenger? *Old Stone Face*
  • Where does Queen Vianne live? *Castle Forte*
  • Describe Castle Fort in three adjectives. *Answers may vary*
  • Who is the queen's lady-in-waiting? *Nicolette*
  • How long has the queen been at Castle Forte? *Two months*
  • How do the guards react to Kaye becoming a knight? *By laughing*
  • Who agrees to be Kaye's mentor? *Beau*

Introduction to a Main Theme: Bravery

  • Introduce the class to the idea of bravery by first asking if anyone can give a definition of the word.
  • Write a basic definition of bravery on the board.
  Bravery: the quality that allows someone to do things that are dangerous or frightening
  • Ask the students to give examples of things that have frightened them.
  Being the new kid at school, going to the dentist, trying a new sport, etc.

- From the examples given, ask students what it would look like to be brave in those situations.
- Ask if anyone has any examples of when they have been brave.
- Ask if students can give examples from the story of when a character is brave.
  When Kaye and Reggie save Beau from the robbers
  When they go before the queen
- Steer the class towards these examples and others, and then ask how the story would have been different if the characters had not been brave.

Activity
Select a few students to come to the front and act out a scene from the story where the characters were brave. Then, have the same students act how the scene would have gone if the characters had not been brave. This is show the class how important it is to be brave in certain situations instead of running away when things are scary.

Vocabulary Activity
Have students select 1-3 words (depending on time restraints) from the vocabulary list, and ask them to write original sentences using the words. Then, ask students to share their sentences (preferably one for each vocabulary word) with the rest of the class, either by writing it on the board or reading it out loud.

Reading Comprehension Questions
- What do Beau and Kaye practice first? *sword fighting*
- Who is the bravest knight to ever live in Knox? *Sir Gregory*
- What was his sword's name? *Celestor*
- What does Beau give Kaye? *A suit of armor*
- What does Beau give Reggie? *a bow*
- How many contests do the knights have to enter in the tournament? *three*
- What is the name of Reggie's position in the final contest? *Squire*
- What was in the two prize purses? *Gold and Tourteletes*
- Who was missing when Reggie and Kaye return home? *Charles*
- How long had he been missing? *two days*
- What had chased Charles up a tree? *a wolf*
- What does Charles name the wolf? *Mungo*

Introduction to a Main Theme: Pride
- Introduce the class to the idea of pride by first asking if anyone can give a definition of the word.
- **Pride:** having too high an opinion of one's own ability or worth : a feeling of being better than others
- Ask students if they can give any examples of when a character is acting prideful
  Melchor is acting prideful when he thinks he is too good to compete against Kaye
  Reggie acts prideful when he doesn't want to help Charles at first
- Ask students what would have happened if Reggie had been too proud to help Charles.
  He may still be stuck in the tree, Kaye might not have been able to save him on his own.

9

Activity

Select a few students to come to the front and act out the scene where Kaye and Reggie are asked to save Charles. Have the student playing Reggie first be too prideful to help, so when Kaye goes to save Charles, Kaye can't bring Charles home. Then, reenact the scene and have Reggie "swallow his pride" and go help Charles. In this version, they are able to bring Charles back, and the rest of the students applaud their bravery.

Vocabulary Activity

Use the vocabulary sentences created by students in the previous class to create a fill-in-the-blank game, by either reading the sentence out loud, leaving out the vocabulary word, or creating a worksheet. Be sure to include a word bank of the vocabulary words either on the board or on the worksheet.

The Lost Castle Treasure

Back of Book Description: The treasure house of Knox castle is empty! Now conspiracy and war threaten the kingdom while mysterious noises and unexplained events fill the castle. As best friends Kaye, Reggie, and Beau search for the missing treasure, jealous knights plot to get rid of Kaye for good. Can Kaye find the treasure in time to save the kingdom? Or will he risk losing his knighthood forever?

Join Kaye, Reggie, and Beau as they search for hidden clues, secret passages, a lost castle treasure, and their place in the world in this fast-paced adventure.

Reading Comprehension Game

Split the class into two teams and keep score on the board, or don't have teams and offer individual students a prize (piece of candy, sticker, etc.) when he or she gets a trivia question right.

- What do Kaye and Reggie call Alfred? *Old Stone Face*
- What does Kaye think prevents him back from being a truly good knight? *The other knights hate him.*
- How does Kaye think he can get everyone at the castle to stop hating him? *By completing a quest*
- Who is Beau? *The duke, Queen Vianne's nephew*
- Who is Oriana? *Beau's Goshawk/Falcon/Bird*
- What skill does Oriana have? *Hunting*
- Who is Nicolette? *Queen Vianne's lady in waiting*
- Who is Alchir? *Reggie, Kaye, and Beau's tutor*
- What does Reggie do to get out of meeting the tutor after dinner? *Pretends to still be hungry*
- What is Kaye's quest? *To find the hidden treasure*
- What does Melchor say Reggie is like? *a dog's tail*
- What are spooks? *ghosts*
- Why is one of the kitchen boys called Tom Spot? *he has freckles*
- Who is the cook? *Abelard*
- How many boys work in the kitchen? *three*
- Which of the boys does not believe in spooks? *Kaye*
- Where do the boys have their lessons? *the library*

Introduction to a Main Theme: Ways to Show Emotion when Writing

Introduce the class to the idea that there are many ways to show emotion without outright saying "I feel happy!" or "I feel sad!" To first illustrate this, have a few volunteer students come to the front of the room to do an acting exercise. Ask the first child to show the class that he or she is excited without using any words. Typical responses will be to jump up and down, clap hands, etc. Then, challenge the next student to show that he or she is excited without words, but in a different way than the first student. See how many different students can come up with different ways to express excitement.

Use examples from chapters 1-11 to reinforce this idea. Read the following passages and having the children decide what emotion is being described. Some of the passages could be a mix of multiple emotions, so there is no one correct answer. Additionally, have the students open to the passages and read along. This will help with reading and reference skills as well as quickly provide context for each segment.

- Page 15: "'Kaye. Look,' I said, croaking like an old frog. I pointed at the thing swaying gently on its string... This time my voice came out high and squeaky, '...it's too dangerous. Someone wants you dead!'"
  Most students will probably answer FEAR.
- Page 29: "I felt like a mace had smashed into my chest. I couldn't breathe. My knees stopped working and I sat down hard on the bed behind me."
  Defeat, Stress, Sadness, Confusion, etc.

- Page 47: "I was alone in the dark with nothing but dust rabbits to protect me from groaning spooks and phantom footprints. I needed to get out of there! I ran wildly back through the dark, away from the spooks and down toward humans—any humans."
  Fear, Startled, Nervous, etc.
- Page 48: "I lay there a moment, wide-eyed, red-faced, and panting."
  Tired, Afraid, etc.
- Page 51: "Just then a gust of wind flapped the open door sharply against the wall with a bang. The boys jumped and yelled."
  Startled, Scared, etc.
- Page 64: "Someone had put some parchment and quills in the middle of the table. My stomach hurt when I saw that…"
  Dread, Disgust, etc.

Introduce Vocabulary for Entire Book:

Either for homework while reading the story, or in class, have each student find one word they do not know in the story and look it up in the dictionary. Use the words and definitions found by the student to create a vocabulary list for all the kids to reference and study as they finish reading the book. OR provide the following list of words for students to look up the definitions of. The following definitions are from the Merriam-Webster Dictionary.

Quiver: (n.) a case for carrying or holding arrows

Prey: (n.) an animal that is hunted or killed by another animal for food

Jumpy: (adj.) very nervous : easily frightened

Humiliate: (v.) to make someone feel very ashamed or foolish

Gravel: (n.) small pieces of rock

Gauntlet: (n.) a glove worn with medieval armor to protect the hand

Stench: (n.) a very bad smell

Logic: (n.) a proper or reasonable way of thinking about or understanding something

Reading Comprehension Game

Like lesson one, create a game to test students on reading comprehension by asking trivia questions.
- Who did Beau write his letter to? *Oriana/his bird*
- Where did Reggie run away to? *The mews*
- What does Reggie keep in his pocket? *A green bead*
- What did the spook fix in the night? *Embert's shirt*
- What is the topic of the book Reggie reads in the library? *Sir Gregory*
- What does the spook leave behind for Embert and then Reggie? *a treat—a sticky honey candy*
- Why doesn't Kaye want anyone's help finding the treasure? *He wants to prove that he is a good knight*
- What does Kaye cut his hands on? *broken glass*
- Who helps mend Kaye's hands? *Nicolette*
- Who finds the hollow spot in the wall? *Tom Spot and Reggie*

Introduction to a Main Theme: Expressing Character Emotions in Writing

Begin by reminding the class that there are many ways to show emotions besides outright saying how you feel. This time, start with reading passages from the selected chapters and having the class guess what emotion is being expressed.

- Page 65: "My stomach felt even worse—like a giant hand had grabbed my guts and started squeezing."
  Sad, Surprised, Shocked, etc. This one might be a giveaway if students read the line below
- Page 67: "I jumped to my feet and glared at Alchir. 'You're just like every other tutor I've ever had. They laugh at me and then leave because I'm stupid. I'm sick of it. This time, I'm leaving first.' I ran out of the library as fast as I could."
  Frustration, Anger, etc.
- Page 114: "I turned around and walked back, clenching my jaw to stop my teeth from dancing against each other. Tom followed a long way behind me, which helped me feel a little more brave, although my knees still quivered like custard."
  Afraid, Nervous, etc.

Activity

Create strips of papers with different emotions fear, happiness, excitement, sadness, etc. and have each student draw one out of a bowl. Then, instruct the children to write a few sentences that express that emotion without using the word. After everyone is finished, call on volunteers to read their writing to the class and have the other students guess what emotion is being described.

Vocabulary Activity

Have students select 1-3 words (depending on time restraints) from the vocabulary list, and ask them to write original sentences using the words. Then, ask students to share their sentences (preferably one for each vocabulary word) with the rest of the class, either by writing it on the board or reading it out loud.

Reading Comprehension Questions

- Who does Reggie run into on his way to the mews? *Milo*
- Name three things that the boys see in the small home they find in the cave.
  Answers will vary, allow three different students to answer.
- What do the boys use to see inside in the cave? *candles/torches*
- Who is the King's "Silent Arrow?" *Delilah/His Falcon*
- What poisoned the King? *the candles*
- Where did Reggie and Beau find Kaye when he went missing? *tied up in the cave*
- Who gets stuck in the rocks in the cave? *Reggie*
- Who ends up being the spook? *Agnes*

Introduction to a Main Theme: Final Reaction to the Book

Start by asking the class what they thought of the end of the book.

- What were their favorite parts?
- Did the story end the way they thought it should?

• Who were the students' favorite characters, and why?

• If students were a certain character in the book, what would they do differently, and why?

Activity

For the final exercise focusing on different ways to express emotion. Have the class maybe in groups or pairs find an example of when an emotion is described in Chapters 23-33. Then decide what emotion is being described and share the passage with the class.

Vocabulary Activity

Use the vocabulary sentences created by students in the previous class to create a fill-in-the-blank game, by either reading the sentence out loud, leaving out the vocab word, or creating a worksheet. Be sure to include a word bank of the vocabulary words either on the board or on the worksheet.

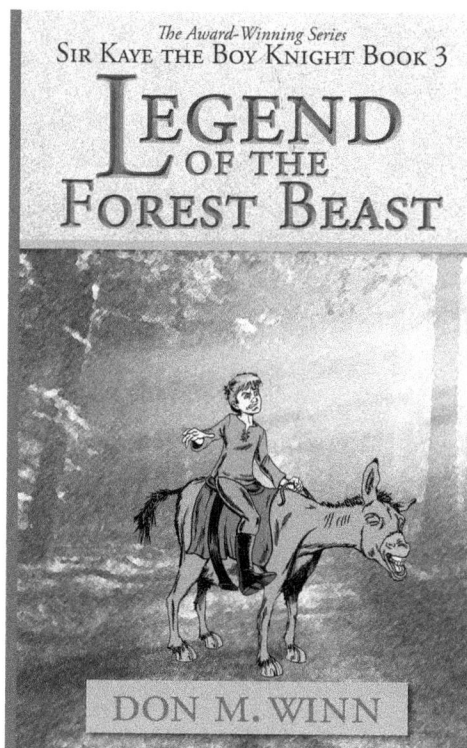

Legend of the Forest Beast

Back of Book Description: The beloved tutor Alchir has vanished!
And a dangerous criminal with a grudge against Alchir has just escaped from prison. Kaye is determined to find the tutor and earn a fine reputation as a knight. The search leads Kaye, Reggie, and Beau to a sinister manor house at the edge of a dark forest where nearby villagers live in terror of a deadly monster. As they investigate the mystery of the forest beast, they uncover a terrible plot that could destroy Knox. When there's no one to turn to for help, can they save the kingdom—and their lives—by themselves?

Reading Comprehension Game

Split the class into two teams and keep score on the board, or don't have teams and offer individual students a prize (piece of candy, sticker, etc.) when he or she gets a trivia question right.

- What do Kaye and Reggie call Alfred? *Old Stone Face*
- Who is Vianne? *The Queen of Knox*
- Who is Beau? *The Duke, Queen Vianne's nephew*
- Who is Alchir? *Reggie, Kaye, and Beau's tutor*
- What was he doing when he went missing? *Going to meet his daughter*
- Why is one of the kitchen boys called Tom Spot? *He has freckles*
- How many boys work in the kitchen? *Three*
- Who is Dworford? *A former knight who escaped from prison, suspected of killing the old king*
- Who is Layla? *Alchir's daughter*
- What kind of mood is Layla in when she arrives at the castle? *Angry, upset, stubborn, etc.*
- What is Layla happy to see when she wakes up? *Her shoes*
- How does Layla describe the man who took her father? *No beard, shield with a hammer design*
- What does Queen Vianne give Reggie? *A blank book to write in*
- What is Reggie's job at Castle Forte? *The Royal Chronicler*
- What does it mean to be the Royal Chronicler? *May vary. He writes down the boys' adventures*
- Why does Reggie think he is wrong for the job? *He's not good at reading and writing*
- What did Layla take with her when he left? *Kaye's horse, Kadar*
- What horse does Reggie ride? *Parsnip*
- What does Kaye end up riding? *A donkey*
- What is the donkey's name? *Grumble*
- Why can't Reggie ride Grumble? *Grumble doesn't like him*
- What shape are the gingerbread treats Reggie has from the kitchen? *Pig-shaped*

Introduction to a Main Theme: Character Creation

In all of the Sir Kaye books, we are introduced to complex and realistic characters. Now the children have a chance to create their own characters. Pass out the character creation sheets, and give the students time to fill in all of the blanks and even draw and color a sketch of their characters. When everyone has had time to complete the worksheet, allow any volunteers to share their work. The character creation sheet can be found at the end of this lesson plan.

Introduce Vocabulary for Entire Book

Either in class or for homework while reading the book, have each student find one word they do not know in the story and look it up in the dictionary. Use the words and definitions found by the students to create a vocabulary list for all the kids to reference and study as they finish reading the book. OR provide the following list of words for students to define using a dictionary.

Landscape: (n.) an area of land that has a particular quality or appearance

Legend: (n.) a story from the past that is believed by many people but cannot be proved to be true

Shrewd: (adj.) being able to understand things and make good judgments : mentally sharp or clever

Steward: (n.) a person whose job is to manage the land and property of another person

Courtly: (adj.) polite and graceful in a formal way

Bridle: (n.) a device that fits on a horse's head and that is used for guiding and controlling the horse

Sneer: (v.) to laugh at someone with an expression on your face that shows dislike and a lack of respect

Flattery: (n.) praise that is not sincere

Attentive: (adj.) thinking about or watching something carefully, paying careful attention to something

Defiance: (n.) a refusal to obey something or someone, the act of defying someone or something

Reading Comprehension Game

Like lesson one, create a game to test students on reading comprehension by asking trivia questions.

- What did the villagers call Kaye? *Sir Donkey*
- What did they call Reggie? *Barleyhead*
- Why did they call him Barleyhead? *Because of his blonde hair, similar in color to ripe barley.*
- What made Grumble like Reggie? *Gingerbread*
- Who did they meet at Dworfurd's manor? *Jake*
- What is Jake's job? *Steward*
- Who is Matilda Glass? *May vary. Woman who lost her husband and daughter to the forest beast*
- What is Matilda's husband's name? *Timothy*
- What is Matilda's daughter's name? *Alys*
- Why is their last name Glass? *Timothy Glass knew how to make glass bottles*
- Who is Bartolemeus/Tolly? *A traveling performer*
- What is his bear's name? *Marigold*
- Why do Kaye and Beau dye Reggie's hair? *So he won't be recognized as Barleyhead*
- What is Reggie's nickname in the kitchen? *Ugly*
- What name does Reggie want to be called by his fellow kitchen workers? *Ben*
- What job had Layla been given by the time Reggie arrived? *A lady's maid for Lady Bragwayne*
- What job does Reggie do for Sir Bragwayne? *Page*

Introduction to a Main Theme: Humility

- Throughout the story, there are many times when the characters have to do embarrassing things or things that make them seem smaller or less important in order to accomplish their goals.
- Ask the class if they can think of any examples of this:

  Kaye riding a donkey instead of Kadar

  Kaye being called Sir Donkey

  Kaye having to deal with the villagers making up mean songs about him

  Reggie having to dye his hair and being called Ugly

  Reggie working in the kitchen and as a page for Sir Bragwayne

- Ask the class if they know what is it called when you lower your own importance to get the job done.
- Introduce class to the word and definition:

  Humility: lowering your own importance to get the job done, not proud, not thinking of yourself as better than other people

- Ask the class if they can think of any examples of what might have happened if the characters hadn't practiced humility:

  Kaye would have never made it out of Castle Forte without riding Grumble

  Reggie wouldn't have been able to get into Bragwayne's manor without dyeing his hair and going to work in the kitchen

- Ask students for examples of times they have practiced humility or could in the future:

  When their little sister wants to play dress up and put crazy makeup all over their faces

  When they are playing sports and have to play a different position than what they want

Activity: Royal Chronicler

At Castle Forte, Reggie has been given the job of the Royal Chronicler, which means he has to write about everything that happens so no one will forget the adventures of Kaye, Reggie, and Beau. Today, give students the chance to document the goings-on of the class. Have the kids go out to playground to play, or even just do activities in the room for ten to fifteen minutes. Then have them write a few sentences about what happened. Don't forget to ask if anyone would like to share their work with the class when everyone is finished.

Vocabulary Activity

Have students select 1-3 words (depending on time restraints) from the vocabulary list, and ask them to write original sentences using the words. Then, ask students to share their sentences (preferably one for each vocabulary word) with the rest of the class, either by writing it on the board or reading it out loud.

Reading Comprehension Questions
- Who first made up the legend of the forest beast? *Bragwayne*
- What did Layla embroider onto Reggie's tunic? *Trout and gnats*
- What did Layla trade for Melchor's help? *Her mother's pearl necklace*
- Where did Kaye hide the treasure? *The cave in the forest*
- What did Reggie THINK he was burning in front of Bragwayne? *The ancient Greek papers*
- Where had Timothy Glass been all along? *In prison*
- Who is Peter Atwood? *Charles's father*
- Whom do they learn is in trouble at the end of the story? *Kaye's father*

Introduction to a Main Theme: Character Analysis
- To begin, ask students to describe Layla in as many adjectives as possible.

  Answers will vary but will mostly likely be along the lines of *pushy, loud, mean, angry, etc.*
- Ask the students to give examples from the story of when she acted in the ways they described.

  When she yelled at the queen, when she called Reggie names, when she stole Kaye's horse, etc.
- Ask students the following questions:

  Would you ever think of yelling at a Queen?

  How did Layla taking Kadar impact Kaye and his dreams?

  Is Layla someone you would like to have as a friend?

21

- Why do you think Layla acts the way she does?

  Answers will vary, but try to steer the class away from the idea that "she is mean."

- Delve deeper into Layla's character. For example consider these facts:

  Layla grew up without a mother, around her father only. How would that have been different from what you have experienced? Would Layla have been different if she had had a mother?

  Sometimes people cry when they get scared or frustrated. Instead, Layla gets angry. Why?

  Did Layla feel or act like she felt helpless when her father was taken away? Why do you so answer?

  Do you think Layla was someone who wanted to jump right in and fix things? Why do you so answer?

- Whenever someone's behavior puzzles us, saddens us, or makes us frustrated, we need to ask a powerful question: **"What was that person feeling or thinking to make acting like they did seem like the right thing to do?"**

- In closing, present Layla's character in this way, then see if the class changes their minds about her. In reality, Layla is a girl with a keen, logical mind, who seeks speedy solutions to her problems, rather than helplessly waiting on others to rescue her or those she cares for. In fact, she makes such quick decisions that she gets frustrated when other people don't come to the same conclusion quickly enough to suit her sense of urgency. However, getting frustrated doesn't help her get the help she needs.

- She needs to work on her communication skills and to be more respectful of people's feelings and possessions, but she is a very strong and loyal character. Even Matty, the kitchen boy, reminds Reggie that when Layla embroidered trout and gnats on Reggie's tunic, she was thinking of them. She even sacrifices the only connection she has with her mother—her precious pearl necklace—to try and save Kaye. She is not afraid of confrontation, boldly speaking up to the queen, Melchor, Jowls, Dworfurd, seeking employment in Bragwayne's manor to help her father, and more. She is a person of action.

- Now how would you answer: **Is Layla someone you would like to have for a friend?**

Vocabulary Activity

Use the vocabulary sentences created by students in the previous class to create a fill-in-the-blank game, by either reading the sentence out loud while leaving out the vocabulary word, or by creating a worksheet. Be sure to include a word bank of the vocabulary words either on the board or on the worksheet.

Character Creation Worksheet

Create your own character! Fill in the blanks below and include any other important information about the character you invent. Then draw your character in the space below. Tell about your character's....

Name and age:

Job:

Friends:

Family:

Where do they live?

Favorite food:

Favorite animal:

Favorite thing to do:

What do they want more than anything?

What are they afraid of?

What else do you want to tell about your character?

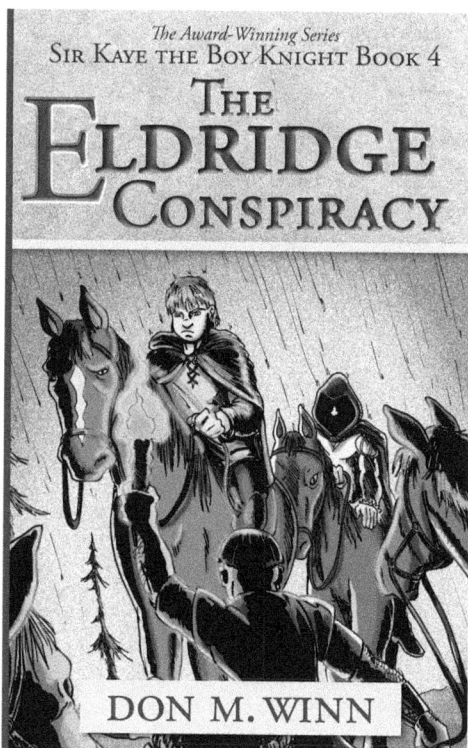

The Eldridge Conspiracy

Back of Book Description: Kaye's father is in danger!

The young knight, Kaye, and his friends Reggie and Beau enter Eldridge in search of the only man who can save Kaye's father. During their journey, they encounter and make a powerful enemy of Baron Thomas—the self-proclaimed heir to the throne of Eldridge—who also has his sights set on ruling the country of Knox. Together, the boys dodge the baron's henchmen and race against time to stop an assassination that would plunge the two kingdoms into war in this exciting conclusion to the series.

Reading Comprehension Game

Split the class into two teams and keep score on the board, or don't have teams and offer individual students a prize (piece of candy, sticker, etc.) when he or she gets a trivia question right.

- What is the name of Reggie's horse? *Parsnip*
- What country do the boys follow Kaye to? *Eldridge*
- What nickname have the people given Kaye? *Sir Donkey*
- Is this a good nickname? *No*
- What had the boys stolen from the baron before the beginning of this book? *Gems*
- Where do the boys find Kaye? *In a churchyard*
- Who lives at an abbey? *Monks*
- What is the name of the abbey the boys visit? *Wislett Abbey*
- What is the name of the man the boys are looking for? *Azam*
- What country are the boys from? *Knox*
- What is the name of Kaye's horse? *Kadar*
- When the boys find Kaye, what has he found at the church? *A letter nailed to the door*
- Under what kind of tree do the boys find Kaye? *An apple tree*
- Who is the first monk the boys meet at the abbey? *Brother Antony*
- What kind of jobs did the monks have at the abbey? *Many were artists and copyists, but they also gardened, cleaned, cooked, and had other jobs, like beekeeping*
- Who is trying to steal the throne from King Aldric? *Baron Thomas*
- How does Baron Thomas plan to ruin King Aldric's good name? *By distributing the placards filled with lies about King Aldric and Sir Henry to all of the cities in Eldridge*
- Where do the monks throw Kaye and Beau? *The abbey cesspit*
- How does Reggie get them out? *He pulls them out with a rope*
- Where does Kaye have a scar? *On his forehead*
- How did he get the scar? *By hitting his head on a rock while training to become a knight*
- How does Kaye plan to help Azam? *By rescuing his wife and daughter*
- What feature makes Azam easy to identify? *He has only one hand*

Introduction to a Main Theme: Future Aspirations

In the first section of Kaye 4, the boys talk about the fact that they can be anything they want to be in life. Take this time to talk to your students about what they might like to be one day. Begin the conversation by asking the following questions, then allow your students to start a discussion:

- Do you believe you can be anything you want to be?
- What do you want to be?
- What do you have to do or learn to accomplish that goal?

Give the class some time to draw a picture of who and what they would like to be in the future.

Introduce Vocabulary for Entire Book

Either for homework while reading the story, or in class, have each student find one word they do not know in the story and look it up in the dictionary. Use the words and definitions found by the student to create a vocabulary list for all the kids to reference and study as they finish reading the book. OR provide the following list of words for students to look up the definitions of. The following definitions are from the Merriam-Webster Dictionary.

Pessimistic: (adj.) seeing the worst, or expecting the worst to happen

Clammy: (adj.) unpleasantly cool and humid

Scowl: (n.) a facial expression of dislike or displeasure

Cowl: (n.) a loose hood or hooded robe

Smother: (v.) extinguish (a fire) by covering it and depriving it of air

Manuscript: (n.) a book, document, or piece of music written by hand rather than typed or printed

Adorn: (v.) to make more beautiful or attractive; to decorate

Treason: (n.) the crime of betraying one's country

Cringe: (v.) to shrink, bend, or crouch, especially in fear

Sickly: (adj.) often ill; in poor health

Reading Comprehension Game

Like lesson one, create a game to test students on reading comprehension by asking trivia questions.

- What is the name of the captain who holds Azam's family captive? *Captain Claymore*
- What is the name of the ship? *The Triumph*
- Who tells Reggie about Captain Claymore? *Theo, a boy Reggie meets on the dock*
- Where does Captain Claymore like to go after being away at sea? *The Swann bathhouse*
- Where does Captain Claymore typically go after his bath? *The alehouse*
- Does the bathhouse owner allow Kaye to buy a bath? *No*
- How often does Captain Claymore take a bath? *Once a month*
- How do Reggie and Kaye manage to sneak around in the bathhouse? *By pretending to work there*
- Where does Captain Claymore keep the key to the ship's cabin? *Around his neck*
- How does Kaye steal the captain's key without him noticing? *Kaye lulls him to sleep, then replaces it with another key*
- How does Reggie distract everyone while Beau and Kaye save Azam's family? *He sets a fire*
- How does Beau signal to Reggie that it is time to start the fire? *He wipes his brow*
- Does Kaye leave Reggie behind on purpose? Why? *Yes, in order to save Azam's wife and child*
- How does Reggie get away from the man chasing him? *Reggie bit him*
- Who is Odessa? *The widow who shelters Azam's family, then houses the boys*
- Where do the boys end up staying the night? *A bakery*
- What do the boys find among the placards? *Two edicts*
- What is peculiar about the edicts? *They contradict each other*
- What do the boys learn that Sir Henry will be doing at the festival? *Jousting against the king*
- What is the king drugged with during the joust? *Poppy syrup*
- Who ends up saving the king's life? *Reggie*

28

Introduction to a Main Theme: Friendship

The importance of friendship is prevalent throughout the series, but especially in this story. Use this time to discuss what friendship means with your students.

Ask the class what friendship means to them.

Ask the class why friendship is so important.

Ask the class what makes a good friend:

- Someone who likes the same things you do, someone who is honest, someone who sticks up for you and supports you, et cetera.

Ask the class if they can think of examples of when the boys showed they were good friends to each other:

- When Reggie and Beau rode through the night to find Kaye.
- When Reggie pulled the boys out of the pit.

Ask the class if they can think of any examples of what might have happened if the boys were not good friends to each other:

- They would not have chased after Kaye to help him.
- Reggie would have not pulled the others out of the pit.
- They would have not worked together to save Sir Henry.

Ask students for examples of how they can be good friends:

- Invite others to join them at lunch or in a game if they are feeling left out.
- Share their games with others and take turns.
- Be there for their friends if someone is upset.

Activity

Throughout the book, Reggie often uses similes to explain how he and his friends feel. Introduce your class to similes, and encourage them to write their own. Below is the definition of a simile, along with some examples and writing prompts to get them started.

Simile: a figure of speech that compares one thing with another of a different kind. The simile is usually in a phrase that begins with "as" or "like."

Examples from the text:

- "I froze, every muscle paralyzed. Sir Henry's words seemed to swirl in the air and drift slowly downward over us, like fat snowflakes falling on a silent graveyard." *Expresses surprise and shock at Sir Henry's words.*
- "He looked disgusted, like he had just stepped on a slimy slug in his bare feet." *Expresses disgust.*
- "Kaye curled his lip like he had seen a repulsive centipede wriggling in his porridge." *Shows disgust.*

Writing Prompts:

- Create a simile that expresses happiness.
- Create a simile that expresses sadness.
- Create a simile that expresses excitement.
- Create a simile that expresses embarrassment.

Vocabulary Activity

Have students select 1-3 words (depending on time restraints) from the vocabulary list, and ask them to write original sentences using the words. Then, ask students to share their sentences (preferably one for each vocabulary word) with the rest of the class, either by writing it on the board or reading it out loud.

Reading Comprehension Questions

- Why is Kaye upset when Sir Henry is proud of Reggie? *Kaye wanted his father to be proud of him*
- Who sits next to Sir Henry during the meal? *Reggie*
- How long does Reggie sleep when he is knocked out? *Fifteen hours*
- Where does Reggie wake up? *In the high tower of King Aethelfred's old castle on the mountain*
- How does Reggie know only Kaye will read his letter? *No one else can read his handwriting*
- Who is Baron Thomas dressed as when he comes to see Reggie? *King Aethelfred*
- What does Reggie find in the throne room? *A trap door*
- Reggie's plan is for Baron Thomas to fall through the trapdoor and get stuck in the stone room. Does it work? *No, he's too big and gets stuck halfway through the trapdoor and he eventually gets out*
- When Kaye comes to rescue Reggie, who is he dressed as? *Sir Donkey*
- What does Reggie use to wake Kaye up when Kaye is knocked out? *Smelly cheese*
- Where does Kaye say the edicts are when he takes Reggie's place? *In his armor*
- What does everyone do when Baron Thomas drags Kaye away? *They throw rocks at him*
- Who started the rock throwing? *Beau*
- What is Reggie's idea to clear Kaye's reputation? *Pretend Sir Donkey was killed in the battle*

Introduction to a Main Theme: Loyalty

Throughout the story, the boys show loyalty in many different ways. Use this time to discuss what loyalty means with your students.

Ask the class what they think loyalty means.

- **Loyalty:** having or showing complete and constant support for someone or something.

Ask the class if they can think of any examples of loyalty from the story:

- When Reggie, Beau and Kaye work so hard to try to save Sir Henry and King Aldric.
- When Kaye comes to save Reggie, even though he was mad at him.
- When the boys stay loyal to the king.

Ask the class if they can think of any examples of characters who were not loyal:

- Baron Tomas, who tries to overthrow the king.
- The monks who abuse their power at the church.

Ask the class for some examples of what might have happened if the boys hadn't practiced loyalty:

- The king and Sir Henry would not have been warned.
- Kaye would not have rescued Reggie.

Ask students for examples of what they are loyal to:

- Family, friends, their school, sports teams, et cetera

Ask students how they show loyalty in their own lives:

- Answers may vary.

Activity

Now that your students have finished reading the book, it is a good time to ask them how they felt about the story. Use some questions to get them started.

- Did they find it interesting?
- Who was their favorite character, and why?
- What was their favorite part of the story?
- What was their least favorite part?
- Would they recommend the book to someone else?

Either as a class or as an individual assignment, give your class time to write reviews of the book. This could even be a typing activity if your students need computer time.

Vocabulary Activity

Use the vocabulary sentences created by students in the previous class to create a fill-in-the-blank game, by either reading the sentence out loud and leaving out the vocab word, or by creating a worksheet. Be sure to include a word bank of the vocabulary words on either the board or the worksheet.

Sir Kaye the Boy Knight Series

Life in the Middle Ages

The following information is designed to help students enjoy an immersive experience during their reading of the *Sir Kaye, The Boy Knight* series of books. Historical material and drawings will provide a frame of reference for a lifestyle so different from the digital existence so prevalent today. There are abundant opportunities for class projects, such as creating coats of arms, experimenting with medieval food, storytelling assignments, knitting demonstrations, field trips to look for herbs in your local area, watching falconry videos from online libraries, and more.

From *The Knighting of Sir Kaye*

Castles

During the Middle Ages, castles were primarily owned by the rich and powerful. This would include royalty (kings and queens), nobility (barons, marquesses, earls, and dukes), and some knights. It was not uncommon for those who were especially rich to own more than one castle. They would divide their time throughout the year among the different castles, traveling from one to another on an extended vacation they called 'going on progress.'

First and foremost, castles were built for protection. However, they served many other purposes. In medieval times, land equated to power. The more land someone had, the more powerful they were. And richer, because they could charge other people rent to live on their land, as well as demand that they help with planting and harvesting crops, thereby increasing the owner's wealth.

Additionally, if someone wanted the owner's power and money, they had to take the owner's land. Castles were a way of protecting one's land and family from anyone who might want to try and take it. They were built to withstand enemy attacks.

Castle Walls

Castle walls played a huge role in protecting the castle in the Middle Ages. The large wall that would surround the entire castle was called the curtain wall, and it was typically built as two parallel walls with a space in between. The area between the two walls was filled with stones (or other leftover building materials they needed to get rid of) to add even more protection and make the wall dense and heavy. When building the walls, the builders would not only build the walls up, but they would dig trenches for deeper foundations, sometimes all the way to bedrock, in order to provide the wall with a sturdy base and to prevent attackers from digging under it.

Castle walls could be up to 28 feet thick. To put that into perspective, an average dinner table is around 8 feet long, so a castle wall would be as thick as 3.5 dinner tables lined up end to end.

Side note: When a castle was under attack, one thing the attackers might do was dig a tunnel starting far away from the castle wall. They would tunnel underground toward the castle wall, building wooden supports to hold up the roof of the tunnel as they went, so it wouldn't fall on them as they were digging. Because they were underground, no one from the castle could shoot arrows at them to stop them, so they could get very close. When they had dug far enough to be right under the castle wall, they would fill the end of the tunnel with straw, hay and pig fat, set it on fire, then run out of the tunnel. The fire would burn through the wooden supports and the tunnel would cave in. When the section of the tunnel right under the castle wall collapsed, many times the castle wall would fall down as well, creating a way for the attackers to get inside. This is where we get the word "undermine." Once the castle wall was down in that spot, the attackers had a way to get inside.

Cut-away View of Castle Wall

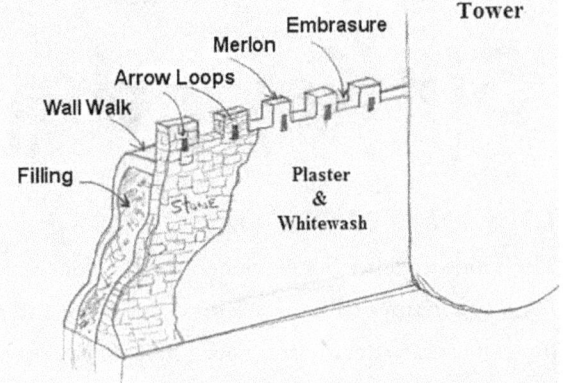

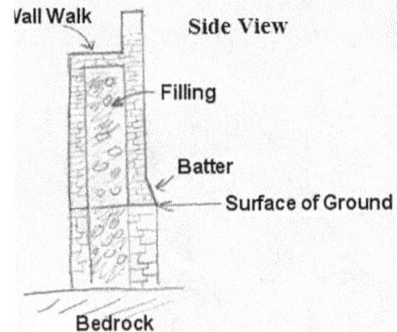

Tower — Embrasure — Merlon — Arrow Loops — Wall Walk — Filling — Plaster & Whitewash

Side View — Wall Walk — Filling — Batter — Surface of Ground — Bedrock

castles as homes

Castle courtyards were like a small village inside the safety of the castle wall. This worked as a way of helping and protecting people when there was an attack or siege on the surrounding area. A siege is when an attacker surrounds a city and cuts off access to outside resources and travel-ways, like roads and rivers. When an attack occurred, all of the villagers would retreat into the confines of the castle walls for safety. In the courtyard area, there were gardens, orchards, animals and even fishponds, to provide everyone with food. Additionally, there was a well where the villagers could get drinking water. Along with food and water, the courtyard also had workshop areas to repair weapons, a blacksmith, and stables to take care of livestock.

When not under attack, castles were simply homes. Cold and drafty homes, since the only heat came from fireplaces, but impressive in their scale and size.

Everyone ate together at the same time, in a room called the great hall, this included the lord and lady, other household members, servants, and workers (except for those serving the meal, of course). It was considered very rude to sneak off and eat privately. The lord and lady of the castle sat with their family at a raised permanent table (on a dais or platform, rather like a stage) at one end of the hall. They sat in big chairs, sometimes with a canopy above their chairs to show how important they were.

Everyone else ate at trestle tables (temporary surfaces that could be put away when it wasn't mealtime). All tables had white cloths on them, and the floor was covered with rushes (dried plants, like straw or hay), sometimes with sweet-smelling herbs like lavender or thyme mixed in. These were added because the floor covering could start smelling pretty bad, since people spilled food, dropped bones leftover from the meat, and

From The Knighting of Sir Kaye

spat on the floor. There were always dogs and cats looking for scraps to eat, and they left things behind, as well. The rushes were changed only a few times a year.

People ate and served themselves with their hands, so it was considered polite to wash before eating, often in bowls of scented water that were brought to the table. There were no knives, forks, and spoons like we have in our kitchens today. Everyone had a personal knife they carried with them everywhere, rather like a pocket knife, which they used to cut off chunks of meat. Plates were called trenchers. Sometimes they were made of wood or a kind of metal called pewter, but many times they were made of thick slices of stale bread. The bread would soak up the juices of whatever was put on them and after the meal, the bread trenchers were sometimes given to poor people as food.

sLeeping arrangements

Beds were very important, and said a lot about a person's wealth and status. Only the wealthiest of the people had them, and they were so important that sometimes they would mention them in their wills so that their children would be sure to inherit such an important piece of furniture. Beds were made to be easily taken apart and put back together again, so the castle owners could take them to their different castles as they moved between them throughout the year.

Beds were constructed of wood, with ropes crisscrossed through holes in the sides of the bedframe to support the mattress. Then there was a feather mattress on top (a big cloth bag filled with feathers). Only the very rich had feather beds, the poor would stuff their mattresses with straw. Sheets, quilts, animal furs, and pillows completed the setup. There were no pillow cases, however. Instead, they had a little piece of cloth that was fastened to the top side of the pillow for their faces to rest on.

Side note: The expression "sleep tight" came from the need to tighten the ropes supporting the mattress from time to time. Saggy ropes did not make for good sleeping. Tight ropes did. However, the expression was not used until the early 1900s.

Some beds also had curtains around them to provide both warmth and privacy. Sleeping arrangements were very different than they are today, and oftentimes, families and servants would share the same room. Sometimes servants slept on a little bed that could be pushed under the Lord's and Lady's big bed during the day. This is what we know today as a trundle bed.

Baths and toiLets

In the Middle Ages, the toilet was referred to as a garderobe. It could be built to project out of a side wall of the castle that was like a balcony over a river, so the sewage would fall into the river and get washed away. However, what usually happened is that the toilet was built into the thickness of the wall, where a chute was hollowed out so the sewage could fall down into a cesspit built into the base of the wall. The cesspit had to be cleaned out every so often because it smelled. The man who cleaned out the cesspit was called a gong farmer, and he emptied it through an opening in the wall near the ground. Hay was used in the way we use toilet paper today.

As you can imagine, garderobes were quite smelly, and people in those times often thought that keeping their woolen clothes in the garderobe would protect them from being eaten by moths. Whether that actually worked or not is debatable, but it certainly couldn't have had a positive effect on the way the clothes smelled.

Side note: Richard the Lionhearted had a castle in France (Chateau Gaillard) that was attacked by enemies (Philip II of France – c. 1204). They got into the cesspit, climbed up the shaft inside the wall and entered the castle through the garderobe.

Baths were taken in a wooden tub lined with cloth or sheets so the people wouldn't get splinters. It was a lot of work to take a bath because servants had to heat the water, then carry it up many stairs to fill up the tub. Every gallon of water weighs eight pounds, and it might take 50 gallons to fill a tub.

Side note: Henry III of England (c. 1216) even had a bath house with hot and cold running water. The water was stored in tanks and could run into a tub for bathing.

Sometimes herbs or perfumes were used to make the water smell nice. Because it was so much work to set up and fill a tub, sometimes family members would take turns in the tub, using the same water.

peasants

Peasants lived close to each other, for protection, in a village, or near a castle. The lord of the castle gave them land to farm for themselves and their families, but in exchange, they had to pay rent and some of them had to work in the castle fields two or three days each week. They could only work their own fields on their days off. Peasant houses were usually one room, and their animals lived inside with them at one end of the house. Sometimes there was a loft.

Houses were built of wattle and daub. Builders used wattle, which was a woven lattice of wooden strips and daub, a sticky mixture of straw, soil, clay, sand, and animal manure, to create earthen walls.

Sometimes everyone in the family shared the bed, which was basically a cloth bag filled with straw, just lying on the floor. This wasn't very nice. It could have bugs or even mice in it, and the straw was only changed about once a year. Little kids might have their own mat to sleep on, or sometimes slept in a loft. They were allowed to sleep in the big bed when they were older.

Peasants didn't usually take baths, especially in cold weather. They would wash their hands and faces regularly, though. Instead of toilets, they might have had an outhouse or a pit outside. Inside, they had a bucket to use for a toilet. It had to be emptied outside, into a pit or a river.

Transportation usually meant walking, however, sometimes an ox with a small cart could be used. Horses were not typically ridden by peasants.

horses

While we have no doubt that Kaye's horse, Kadar, was a big and strong steed, typically in the Middle Ages, horses were smaller than most of the horses we see today. They were also a very important part of medieval life and were used for war, farming, and transportation. Medieval horse owners rarely differentiated horses by breed, but instead, they were set apart and identified by the job they did.

The three main horse types in the Middle Ages were "chargers" (war horses), "palfreys" (riding horses), and cart or packhorses.

From *The Knighting of Sir Kaye*

36

knights

A knight's primary job was to help their lord defend his land. And since land was power, the knight's job was very important. A knight defended the castle, his lord, and the people of the area. He was also responsible for fighting off invaders.

Tournaments were used as a way for the knights to practice their sword-play and other skills.

There were two ways to become a knight. The first involved a process of training and learning.

The steps toward knighthood:

- Become a Page: At age seven, a nobleman's son began training for knighthood. They were sent away to the castles and homes of wealthy lords or relatives to embark on their knighthood training. As a page, a boy learned how to fight, how to use weapons, and how to ride a horse into battle. He learned manners from the nobleman's wife. Like everyone, pages had a strict rule of conduct, and a certain way of behaving that they had to follow.

- Become a Squire: At age 15, a page could become a squire, and each squire was assigned to a knight. A knight could have several squires and each assisted the knight to whom he was assigned. Squires continued to learn how to fight as well as how to behave chivalrously.

- Be Knighted: Once a squire proved himself in battle, and his knight felt he was ready, he could become a knight himself. Squires were knighted in elaborate ceremonies.

The second way a person could be made a knight was for a king, queen, or even another knight to bestow knighthood as a reward for a courageous act.

From *The Knighting of Sir Kaye*

chivalry

Chivalry was the medieval code of conduct that a knight was expected to follow. Chivalry included such things as bravery, honor, courtesy, respect, protection of the weak, generosity, and even fairness to enemies.

Many may ask if chivalry exists today. While the statement that "chivalry is dead" is typically made as a reference to men not holding the door for women, the concept of chivalry goes much deeper than that. As we see above, the definition of chivalry encompasses all of the attributes necessary to be a good citizen, friend, family member, sportsman, and person. The need for chivalry can be seen in all aspects of modern life.

medieval food

In medieval times the poorest of the poor might survive on garden vegetables, including peas, onions, leeks, cabbage, beans, turnips (also called swedes), and parsley. A staple food of the poor was called pottage—a stew made of oats and garden vegetables with a tiny bit of meat in it, often thickened with stale bread crumbs. Brown bread made from rye, barley, or oats was eaten in most homes on a regular basis. When it got stale, it was crumbled and used to thicken soups and stews. The stale bread could also be cut into thick slices and used as plates called trenchers. Nothing was wasted. Manchet, or white bread made from wheat, was usually only eaten by the wealthy.

Fresh milk did not last long in the Middle Ages because there was no refrigeration. So milk was made into cheese that had a shelf life of several months. Instead of fresh milk, some wealthier households used nut milk—ground almonds or walnuts boiled and strained through a sieve. The liquid collected was used as a substitute for milk in soups, main dishes, and desserts.

Many households raised chickens, ducks, or geese for eggs and eventually for meat, but only after the bird had stopped laying eggs. These birds were far more valuable as egg-producers than as meat for the table.

The homes of the nobility often had "deer parks," which were wooded areas where the gentry could hunt for sport and food. Peasants who poached game (hunted without permission) on these reserves were punished severely, or sometimes even put to death if caught. One exception to this severe punishment was the hunting of rabbits—a peasant caught poaching rabbits was subject to only a small fine.

Poor people could not afford spices. Spices were rare and very expensive because they didn't grow in England or nearby Europe, coming instead from far islands that were many months away by boat. Peasant foods were more often flavored with onions, garlic, and herbs like parsley and sage that they could grow in their garden or forage for in the fields and woods.

The more well-to-do would enjoy spices such as pepper, cinnamon, mace, nutmeg, saffron, grains of paradise, cloves, ginger, and galangal. Do some of those sound exotic? Grains of paradise are seeds that have a pepper-like flavor. Galangal is similar to ginger.

From *Legend of the Forest Beast*

Spices were precious, and were guarded like jewels. Wealthier people that had spices kept them locked up, and the lady of the house carried the key attached to her belt at all times. Once a day she would venture to the kitchen to measure out the day's ration of spices for the cook.

Experimentation with varieties of herbs and spices was not a well-established art; instead, spices were frequently used in combinations that would be unlikely for today's palates. For example, in our day, when we think of cinnamon, we think of cinnamon rolls, cinnamon toast, or maybe oatmeal cookies. But in the past, cinnamon was mainly used for flavoring meat dishes. Spices were something of a status symbol, and the more you had, the more you used, and people were duly impressed.

Honey was the most common sweetener in the Middle Ages. Although sugar was available in many forms in medieval times, it was used sparingly because of its expense. It was viewed as more of a spice than a sweetener, especially for meat sauces. If you think it's gross to have sugar in your meat sauce, think for a minute about ketchup and barbeque sauce—both of those have plenty of sugar in them. Sugar was also stirred into wine to make it more palatable.

knitting

While knitting is considered a hobby among women in contemporary culture, back in Kaye's day, knitting would have been an activity and profession of men. Men even had their own knitting guilds, or professional associations, so it makes sense that Kaye would have learned his knitting skills from his grandfather. Knitted goods were also the most popular among men, as knitted tights had more stretch than the alternatives, and were less likely to sag around the knees. Women were still wearing long skirts, so they had less of a need for fashionable hosiery than the men did.

From *The Lost Castle Treasure*

38

HeraLòry

In simplistic terms, heraldry is the study and creation of coats of arms. Just as modern sports players have their names and numbers on the backs of their jerseys, knights decorated their armor with designs so that people could recognize them. Historically, there doesn't seem to be any reliable explanation for why certain designs or animals were chosen to be part of a coat of arms. It seems that the owner of the coat of arms just chose whatever they liked. For example, one person could include a lion in their coat of arms, saying that it stood for bravery and courage, while another person could have a lion on theirs and say that it stood for nobility and royalty. And both of them would be right.

Sometimes shields had patterns on them. These patterns are called variations. A shield could have variations over the whole shield or only on part of it. The patterns are usually made with two colors.

- Barry – horizontal (sideways) stripes
- Paly – vertical (up and down) stripes
- Bendy – diagonal stripes
- Chequy – a pattern of squares, like a checkerboard
- Lozengy – a pattern of diamonds, like a diagonal checkerboard
- Chevronny – a stripe-like pattern of upside-down v-shapes

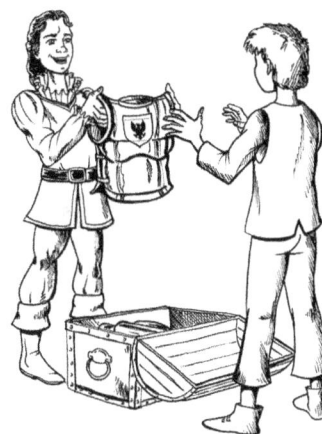

From *The Knighting of Sir Kaye*

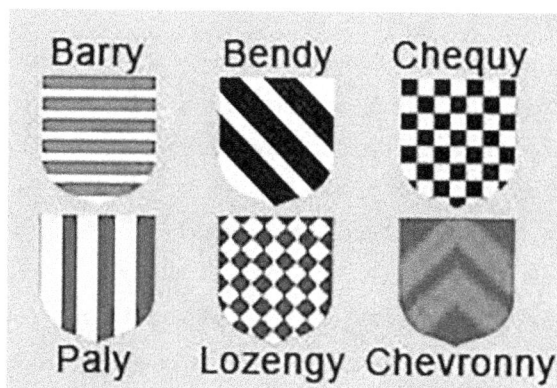

faLcons

Falconry is the art of training birds of prey (raptors) such as falcons, hawks, or even eagles to hunt along with a person. It was an important part of medieval life—a well-trained goshawk could be a main contributor to the family diet. At the beginning of the Middle Ages, falconry was less of a sport and more of a means of providing food for the table.

Note on falconry terminology: Birds of prey are known as raptors. Raptors commonly used in hunting include both falcons and hawks. Today the term falconry refers to the training and flying of any type of raptor. Falconers (those who practice the art of falconry) call their raptors hawks even if their raptor is technically a falcon.

A hawk, even a trained hawk, is not a pet but a wild animal. A falconer may love the hawk, but the hawk doesn't love the falconer back. The hawk sees it as more of a working relationship.

From *The Lost Castle Treasure*

The hawk tolerates the falconer because there is a benefit in doing so. The benefit is that the hawk is well fed and well cared for. That is why a hawk, despite being completely free to fly away at any time during a hunt, usually returns to the falconer. The hawk knows it would be giving up its easy meals if it left.

storyteLLing

Storytelling was probably even more important in medieval society than it is now. There were no movies or television. There were no newspapers or radio to get the news, no computers or internet. Most people learned about their world by telling each other about it. Story books were very rare, so kids would look forward to hearing stories, even more than they do now!

From *Legend of the Forest Beast*

Professional storytellers were people who traveled from town to town. Because they were very good at telling stories, they could receive food, lodging and items of value in exchange for the stories they would tell.

Every storyteller was different. Some could also sing, play a musical instrument or recite poetry. Each one had their own style and talents.

There are different names for storytellers, depending on their skills and what country they came from. English or Welsh storytellers may have been known as bards, while storytellers in Scandinavia may have been known as skalds. Musical storytellers in France may have been known as troubadours.

Medieval storytellers would seek out noble families with a castle or a large country manor. They sought wealthy people who had the means to reward them for their stories. A good storyteller always had an honored place by the fire or near the dinner table. They were welcome guests!

archery

The training of a medieval bowman was very time-consuming, as the archer had to learn to be very precise. The first arrows used were called "broad heads." These arrows, like the name suggests, had a very large head that would provide an impact over a large surface. These arrows did not work well to pierce armor or chain mail, and would often break upon impact. This problem was solved with the smaller and sleeker "bodkin" arrows that worked to pierce armor and chain mail easily. However, with new arrows came a whole new method of archery, and all master archers had to relearn their craft to properly use the new arrows.

From *The Knighting of Sir Kaye*

Ladies' maids

The primary job of the ladies' maid was to look after the lady of the house. On an average day, typical chores would be to lay out her clothes, help her dress, run her bath, do her errands, comb and arrange her hair, and serve as a confidant and friend. Ladies maids were seen as a cut above the rest of the household servants, and were often allowed much more freedom with their choice of dress than the rest of the household servants. They also spent a lot of time sewing. All clothing was made by hand, and while the garments of the rich were usually made by special dressmakers, ladies' maids often made undergarments for the family or sewed shirts to donate to the poor. Needlepoint was an important skill for women as well. Tapestries, altar cloths, and decorative pillows contributed to a beautiful environment inside the cold stone walls of castles and churches.

Child Labor

In the middle ages, it was not uncommon for a child as young as ten to begin pushing a plow in his father's field, or to begin an apprenticeship. Apprenticeships were when a young person went to work side by side with someone skilled and experienced, perhaps considered a master of their craft. Blacksmiths, draftsmen, stonemasons, shoemakers, dressmakers, musicians, and toolmakers were all desirable as mentors to an apprentice.

education

In the Middle Ages, only about 5% of the population was literate. Some lords actually liked it that way and would create laws forbidding their servants from reading and writing. Education was only for the sons of rich families. Grammar schools were usually part of a large church, where boys would be schooled in reading, writing, logic (defending their viewpoint on a topic), and rhetoric (public speaking). Girls were either taught by tutors at home or by their mothers, or a hired woman called a governess. Common areas of study for girls were writing, music, dancing, conversation, elegant manners, and needlework.

books

Medieval books were all handmade, so each one was different. The covers were often made of leather or wood and may have been decorated with paint or gems. The pages were made from a thin form of leather known as vellum. Later, books had paper pages. Many books were liturgical (religious), medical, scientific or philosophical; and others included famous stories, poems or legends of the past. Many were written in Latin, and others were written in the local languages of the time.

Medieval books were expensive, so they were usually purchased by the church or noble families. There were no public libraries. Most people could not read, even those who owned books!

Those who could read might become teachers, physicians, geographers, astronomers, engineers or mathematicians. Reading was a doorway to the universe, just as it is today.

From *The Lost Castle Treasure*

medieval medicine

First Aid: Common first aid in the middle ages typically consisted of washing the wounded area in whatever was nearby. This included water, beer, wine, and vinegar. Minor cuts were smeared with honey, which is now known to have strong antibiotic properties. However, most minor injuries were usually left alone.

Injuries and Wounds: Major wounds were flooded with water or vinegar, packed with herbs and poultices, and then wrapped in strips of cloth. Ligation (sewing) of the wound was not unknown, and was practiced with regular sewing thread before the invention of catgut. Catgut was not made, as it sounds, from the guts of cats. It was actually made from sheep, cow, or goat intestines, which contain a collagen fiber that was used, along with a needle, to sew wounds closed. Honey, again, might be smeared onto the wound. Cautery (touching the wound with red-hot metal) was sometimes used to seal wounds and stop bleeding, especially after amputation.

The setting of broken bones was an art practiced throughout generations. Sometimes a Barber-Surgeon did bone setting, but most often it was an art unto itself. If broken bones were not properly set, infection could set in and cause early death. King Tut, the ancient Egyptian Pharaoh, is one example of such an early death, and it is widely held that England's King Henry VIII with his never-healed jousting wound might be as well. A bonesetter would carefully palpate (feel by hand) the area first to size up the situation, and then draw and pull the limb to align the bones. Then the broken limb would be wrapped in flannel strips and sometimes packed in comfrey paste (which formed a hard cast when dried) or cast with mud or wheat paste.

From *The Lost Castle Treasure*

Treating Infections: Local healers or wise women grew or found herbs to make soothing teas or tisanes (herbal remedies.) Common ingredients were mint, licorice root, willow-tree bark (the basis for modern aspirin) and others, depending on the area and time of year. Unfortunately, it was common to treat fevers as a "chill" and smother the patient under blankets in a stuffy room with a hot fire in the fireplace. Many died of dehydration. Leeches were sometimes used to draw the "evil humours" from the patient's body.

41

Side note: "Evil humours" were the ancient Greek basis for medicine, the belief that blood, phlegm, black bile and yellow bile were the four fluids responsible for controlling a person's health. These were in turn associated with the fundamental elements of air, water, earth and fire. It was further proposed that each of the humours was associated with a particular season of the year, during which too much of the corresponding humour could exist in the body. Blood, for example, was associated with spring. A good balance between the four humours was essential to retain a healthy body and mind, as imbalance could result in disease. Many diseases were considered to be caused by an excess of blood, creating a need for "blood-letting." The instrument used to draw the blood was called a fleam, and it is can still be seen today on many medical symbols. Blood-letting was also used to treat fevers. Medicine didn't change until the 1800's when germs were discovered.

Dental Care: Barber-Surgeons would extract rotten teeth by first wiggling them loose and then pulling them out with plier-like forceps. Otherwise, people would clean their teeth and try to freshen breath by chewing herbs like peppermint and rosemary, rinsing the mouth with vinegar or a solution made of herbs, and rubbing the teeth with coarse material like cheese-cloth. There were no toothbrushes or toothpastes. They used twigs as toothpicks.

abbeys in the middle ages

In the Middle Ages, an abbey was a group of buildings near a church that housed the monastics (the buildings were also sometimes called a convent, friary, nunnery, monastery, or priory). **Monastics**, or people who adopted the monastic way of life, were individuals who chose to renounce all worldly pursuits and devote themselves strictly to spiritual works. Typically, we hear them called **monks** or **nuns**. Commonly, abbeys were either inhabited only by females and run by an **abbess**, or they were strictly male and run by an **abbot**. Rarely, there were double monasteries, which housed men and women, and those were led by an abbess as well.

Life at the Abbey. Life at the abbey was very simple. Days consisted of worship services, reading the Bible, and hard labor. There was little staff; the monks or nuns were the staff, so everyone had to do their part to maintain the abbey. Days were spent farming and raising all of the supplies (farm animals, vegetables, grains) needed to feed everyone who lived there, or cooking, cleaning, sewing necessary garments and linen, and doing laundry chores. The first worship service of the day usually began around 2 a.m., and the last service would conclude the day at sunset.

Monastics would also spend time during the day or night reading the Bible, praying, singing or chanting, and meditating for hours.

There are modern-day monasteries, where the pattern of life is basically similar to life in an abbey during the Medieval era. In modern-day monasteries, monks do all of their own farming and cleaning and live very basic lives, so they can be sure to keep their priorities on spiritual things. Even their food choices are simplified in order to prevent greed or gluttony; they choose to eat bland things that work to sustain them and keep them healthy, rather than rich or highly spiced foods that many of us would prefer.

From *The Eldridge Conspiracy*

From *The Eldridge Conspiracy*

Uses for an Abbey. Abbeys filled many needs in their community, serving as farms, inns, hospitals, schools, and libraries. Abbeys would give travelers and pilgrims a place to stay for the night, and monks and nuns would never turn away a sick person who came to their door seeking help. Most abbeys had a skilled herbalist among its residents who could minister to the needs of the sick or injured. Additionally, the monasteries would provide education for young boys who wished to become priests. Some monastics spent time copying manuscripts of important books so that they could be preserved, and they kept records of important events that happened in their communities. Like Reggie, the residents of Abbeys were often chroniclers

Conspiracies in Abbeys. The following is a matter of history. Nearing the end of the Middle Ages, there was a problem with serious corruption in the church. All members of the clergy were supposed to be well-educated; however, many priests and leaders were illiterate. There were some who hardly knew how to perform the religious services. Many took advantage of their positions and used them to live materialistic and luxurious lives. They convinced pilgrims that the holy relics at their abbeys had the power to cleanse them of their sins, and then charged the pilgrims to see the relics. To make it worse, some of these "relics," which were said to be things like pieces of Jesus' cross, Moses' burning bush, or straw from Jesus' manger, were nothing but things these monks and priests had found on the ground.

These corrupt leaders' most profitable form of income was selling indulgences. An indulgence was a piece of paper signed by the Pope that was a "get out of jail free card" of sorts. A person could cash in an indulgence to be forgiven for one sin. Some clergy even taught that through indulgences, salvation could be attained—if one bought enough indulgences.

jousting

What is jousting and how did it get its start? Jousting is derived from Old French word *joster*, ultimately from Latin *iuxtare*, meaning "to approach, to meet." And "to meet" is exactly what happens in jousting. Jousting is the sport in which two knights fight on horseback while holding heavy lances, with each opponent endeavoring to strike his opponent while riding towards him at high speed, and if possible, breaking the lance on the opponent's shield or jousting armor, or unhorsing him.

The lance was made of wood with a metal tip made of steel or iron and measured between 9 and 14 feet in length. The participants experienced over three times their body weight in G-forces when the lances collided with their armor.

The beginnings of jousting did not look like what we imagine today. Originally, there was no divider between the two competitors, and the jousters would run straight at each other with their lances. As one could imagine, this head-to-head combat on horseback led to many injuries and fatalities. However, the introduction of the divider created a more controlled battleground.

From *The Eldridge Conspiracy*

A list was the field or arena where a jousting event was held and a divider, which was initially just cloth stretching along the center of the field, eventually became a wooden barrier known as the tilt.

Jousting started as a form of weapons training that became popular in the Middle Ages as a result of heavy cavalry (armored men on war horses) becoming the primary weapon of the time. First, jousting was simply a way of training knights for battle in a controlled environment. The sport taught new knights horsemanship, accuracy, and how to react in combat. However, what was created as a military training exercise quickly became a popular form of entertainment.

The first recorded jousting tournament was said to be arranged by a Frenchman named Godfrey de Preuilly in 1066, and tournaments soon became so popular the king had to put a limit on how many tournaments could be held, so that not all of the knights would be busy jousting when a real conflict arose.

Jousting tournaments were considered highly formal events, and they were planned and arranged months in advance. After gaining the proper royal permits, nobles would challenge their neighboring landowners, and each would choose their best knights to fight. (Nobles owned the land during the middle ages. Knights served the nobles who owned the land, helping to defend and protect it. Sometimes a knight could own land himself. It was often granted as a reward for his good work as a knight.) Sometimes, during a tournament, a noble would hire a man to joust for his "team" who was not a knight committed to that noble's land. These knights were called "freelancers," which is where we get the term today.

By the 14th century, jousting became very popular with many members of the nobility, including kings. Jousting was a way to showcase their own skill, courage, and talents, and the sport was just as dangerous for a king as a knight. England's King Henry VIII suffered a severe injury to his leg when a horse fell on him during a tournament, ending the 44-year-old king's jousting career and ultimately leaving him with wounds from which he never fully recovered.

King Henry II of France was the most famous royal jousting fatality. During a jousting exhibition to celebrate the marriage of his daughter to the king of Spain in 1559, the king received a fatal wound when a sliver of his opponent's lance broke off and pierced him in the eye.

Many aspects of jousting tournaments mirror the sports customs we still have today. For instance, medieval heralds would work similarly to sports journalists of the day, promoting the events and jousters. Many of the best jousters became very famous, like today's sports heroes. It became such a popular form of entertainment that jousters would travel around on jousting circuits, fighting each other over and over.

Knights did not just compete for fame and bragging rights. They often competed for gifts, money, and possibly even land from a grateful noble.

From *The Eldridge Conspiracy*

From *The Eldridge Conspiracy*

ships in the middle ages

What were cog ships and what role did they play in medieval times? A cog ship, also simply known as a "cog" was a large, spacious transport ship used in the Middle Ages. The first written history of cog ships dates back to 948 AD in Amsterdam. When cog ships were first created, they had open hulls (the body of the ship) and could only be rowed short distances. The 13th century saw great advancements in technology for cog ships, which resulted in larger ships with decks, raised platforms, bows, and sterns. Additionally, rudders began to appear on cog ships around 1240 AD. Cog ships gradually replaced the traditional Viking ships in northern Europe. The upgraded ships led to increased exploration, conquest, and military ventures.

Since there was no photography during the Middle Ages, no one is exactly sure what a cog ship looked like back in its day. Our best guesses come from images of the time, such as those that were found on seals (carved images that were used by pressing them into hot wax to make an impression) that featured cog ships. The best-preserved cog ship existing today, the Bremen cog, dates from 1380. The wreckage of the Bremen cog was found buried in a river in Germany in 1962. However, even on the Bremen cog, only the hull is preserved, while the rig (mast and mast machinery) is gone.

When cog ships were first created, they could only travel very slowly and for short periods of time. But gradually refinements and improvements were made, and by the 13th century, cog ships were strong enough to cross even the most dangerous of oceans, and were equipped to be protected from pirates. Some were even used as warships.

From *The Eldridge Conspiracy*

By the 14th century, cog ships were slowly phased out by a new kind of ship called the hulk ship.

Features that are common for all cog ships include: One single square sail, **clinker** outer planking at the sides of the hull, straight steep stem and sternposts (opposed to the rounded Viking stem), relatively flat bottoms, and strong cross-beams, usually protruded through the ships' sides, holding the sides together.

Note: Clinker, also known as lapstrake, is a method of boat building where the edges of hull planks overlap.

The cog ship in The Eldridge Conspiracy is a merchant ship called the *Triumph*. Compared to older ships modeled after Viking vessels, the cog ship was well-suited for a merchant vessel because of its higher capacity for carrying cargo. The Triumph includes all the design advancements made by the 13th century.

Other than very old and rare cog ship wreckage that has been found, there are no actual cog ships still in existence from the time period. However, if you ever travel to Europe, especially Sweden and Germany, you can find some working recreations of cogships that actually sail, and you can pay to take a ride in them.

Video reference: You can search YouTube for a video called Hanseatic Cog at Sea. It's a recording of a recreated medieval cog ship called Twekamp af Elbogen arriving at Falsterboro canal in Sweden.

john of gaunt, duke of Lancaster, a historical conspiracy

An actual historical event inspired an aspect of The Eldridge Conspiracy. In England, Parliament had assembled on January 27, 1377, with Crown Prince Richard of Bordeaux and his uncle, John of Gaunt, Duke of Lancaster, presiding. Disturbing rumors spread throughout Parliament that John of Gaunt was a changeling (not born of noble blood, but substituted as a baby for the real royal infant, who had died). These rumors were causing "great noise and great clamor" throughout the assembly. The rumors were not true. They appear to have been spread by the banished Bishop William of Wykeham in an attempt to topple the duke. The duke was a target because of his power over the young prince.

The bishop asserted (falsely) that John of Gaunt's mother, Queen Philippa, actually gave birth to a daughter but "overlaid and suffocated" her. Fearful of confessing this to King Edward, she had another infant smuggled into St. Bavoon's Abbey and replaced her dead daughter with this living child, the son of a Ghent laborer, butcher, or porter. She named the child John and brought him up as her own. Philippa was said to have admitted this in confession to Bishop William of Wykeham on her deathbed in 1369, insisting that should there ever arise any prospect of John succeeding to the throne, the bishop must break the seal of the confessional and publicly reveal the truth.

In The Eldridge Conspiracy, Baron Thomas attempts to spread a similar nasty rumor about King Aldric, hoping that it will help him in his attempt to take the throne from King Aldric.

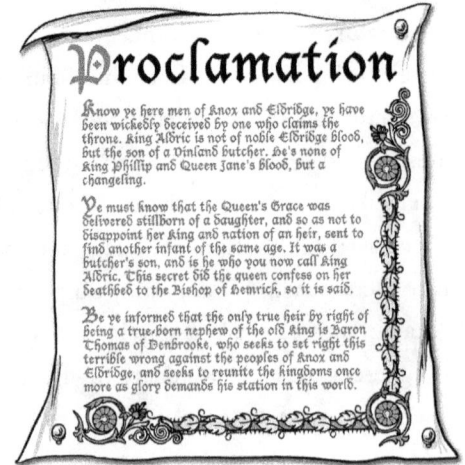

Proclamation

Know ye here men of Knox and Eldridge, ye have been wickedly deceived by one who claims the throne. King Aldric is not of noble Eldridge blood, but the son of a Vinland butcher. He's none of King Phillip and Queen Jane's blood, but a changeling.

Ye must know that the Queen's Grace was delivered stillborn of a daughter, and so as not to disappoint her King and nation of an heir, sent to find another infant of the same age. It was a butcher's son, and is he who you now call King Aldric. This secret did the queen confess on her deathbed to the Bishop of Henrick, so it is said.

Be ye informed that the only true heir by right of being a true-born nephew of the old King is Baron Thomas of Denbrooke, who seeks to set right this terrible wrong against the peoples of Knox and Eldridge, and seeks to reunite the kingdoms once more as glory demands his station in this world.

From The Eldridge Conspiracy

Check out Don Winn's Cardboard Box Adventures blog for more details and medieval research.
You can access Don's CBA blog from the www.donwinn.com website.
© 2017 Don Winn